COMHAIRLE

ENVIRONMENTAL
ISSUES

BookLife
PUBLISHING

By Emilie Dufresne

BookLife
PUBLISHING

©2019
BookLife Publishing Ltd.
King's Lynn
Norfolk, PE30 4LS

ISBN: 978-1-78637-602-2

Written by:
Emilie Dufresne

Edited by:
Kirsty Holmes

Designed by:
Amy Li

CONTENTS

PAGE 4   What Is Mining?

PAGE 6   Types of Mining

PAGE 8   Effects of Mining

PAGE 10   Mining Disasters

PAGE 12   Mining Facts

PAGE 14   What Is Deforestation?

PAGE 16   Types of Deforestation

PAGE 18   Effects of Deforestation

PAGE 20   Deforestation Disasters

PAGE 22   Deforestation Facts

PAGE 24   Glossary and Index

Words that look like **this** can be found in the glossary on page 24.

WHAT IS MINING?

Mining is the process of taking materials out of the ground that are useful or worth a lot of money. Lots of different materials can be mined.

Some materials that are mined include:

FUELS SUCH AS COAL

PRECIOUS METALS SUCH AS GOLD AND SILVER

PRECIOUS STONES SUCH AS SAPPHIRES AND DIAMONDS

TYPES OF MINING

STRIP MINE

Mining can be done in different ways depending on how deep the material is underground. If the material is close to the surface, mines can either be dug in strips across the land, or in a large pit or hole.

Mining deep underground is called sub-surface mining. A hole is dug straight down to where the material starts. This is called a shaft. **Horizontal** tunnels are then dug to get to the rest of the material. These are called adits.

SHAFT

ADIT

EFFECTS OF MINING

Mining can be very bad for the **environment**. Surface mining digs up a lot of the ground where plants and animals live. This destroys **habitats** and food sources.

THIS AREA WAS ONCE A FOREST WHERE LOTS OF ANIMALS AND PLANTS LIVED.

Mining also releases harmful **chemicals** into the water and air around the mine. This can make water unsafe to drink. It can also cause acid rain which can damage forests, rivers and lakes.

MINING DISASTERS

Mining is a very dangerous job. Every year there are lots of mining accidents that harm both humans and the environment.

IN 2015, A BRAZILIAN MINE ACCIDENTALLY RELEASED ITS DANGEROUS WASTE MATERIALS INTO THE SURROUNDING AREA.

MINE

BENTO RODRIGUES VILLAGE

A dangerous mixture of water, mud and chemicals flooded the village of Bento Rodrigues. This accident **contaminated** a very large area with water containing harmful metals. This affected lots of plants, animals and humans.

MINING FACTS

The deepest surface mine in the world is Bingham Canyon, located in Utah in the US. It is over 1.2 kilometres deep.

THAT'S ABOUT THREE TIMES AS TALL AS THE EMPIRE STATE BUILDING!

When coal is burned, it releases dangerous **greenhouse gases** such as carbon dioxide. When burned, coal releases more carbon dioxide than any other fuel.

COAL IS A MATERIAL THAT IS OFTEN MINED. IT IS BURNED TO RELEASE HEAT AND POWER.

WHAT IS DEFORESTATION?

Deforestation is when a large area of plants and trees are cleared. This is done so that the land can be used for other purposes.

DEFORESTATION OF PINE TREES

PALM OIL CROPS GROWING IN A FOREST

Deforestation creates space for other industries such as logging, farming and mining.

TYPES OF DEFORESTATION

Different types of deforestation are used depending on what the space will be used for. If the land is being used for logging, certain trees may be cut down, while others are left to grow. This is a **sustainable** way of deforesting.

Clearcutting involves removing all plant and animal life from an area so that nothing is left. Sometimes this land is then burned to **fertilise** the soil for crops. This is called slash-and-burn deforestation.

THESE METHODS ARE BAD FOR THE ENVIRONMENT.

SLASH-AND-BURN DEFORESTATION

EFFECTS OF DEFORESTATION

Trees do the very important job of storing harmful gases like carbon dioxide and creating helpful gases like oxygen. When they are cut, trees release the carbon dioxide they were storing and can no longer change carbon dioxide into oxygen.

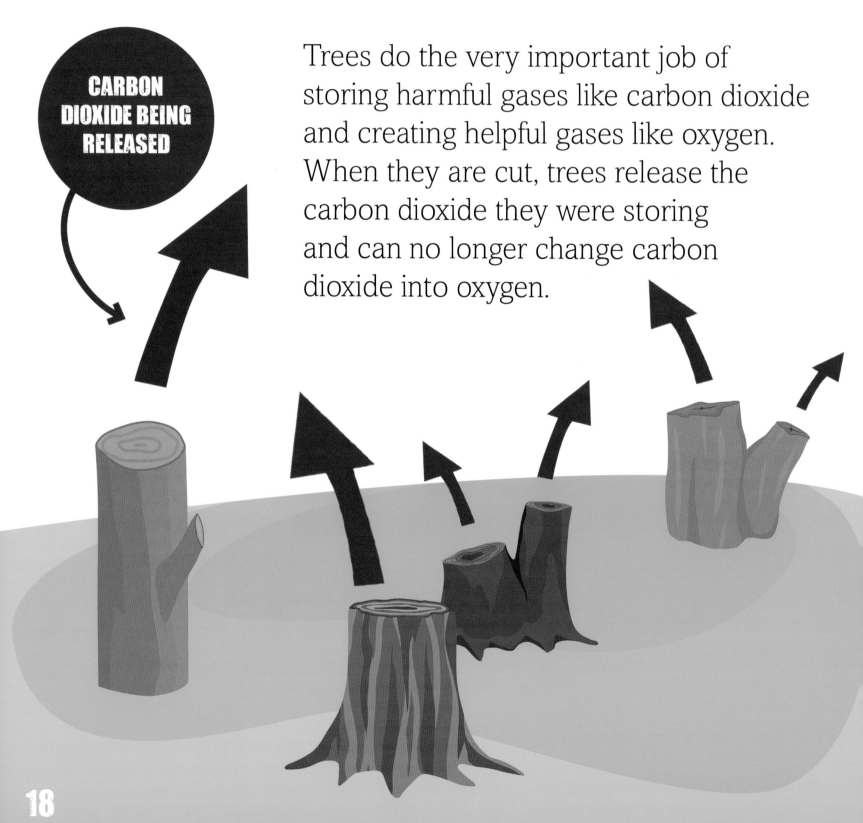

CARBON DIOXIDE BEING RELEASED

Carbon dioxide is a type of greenhouse gas. Greenhouse gases are bad for the environment because they trap heat from the Sun and add to global warming.

GLOBAL WARMING CAUSES PROBLEMS SUCH AS EXTREME WEATHER, RISING SEA LEVELS AND EXTINCTION OF DIFFERENT SPECIES.

DEFORESTATION DISASTERS

Global warming isn't the only thing that deforestation leads to. It can also can cause flooding and turn areas of fertile land into deserts. This is called desertification.

Deforestation also causes plant and animal habitats to be lost. This can make certain species endangered or extinct. For example, many animals in the Sumatran rainforest are in danger of losing their habitats and becoming extinct, such as the Sumatran tiger.

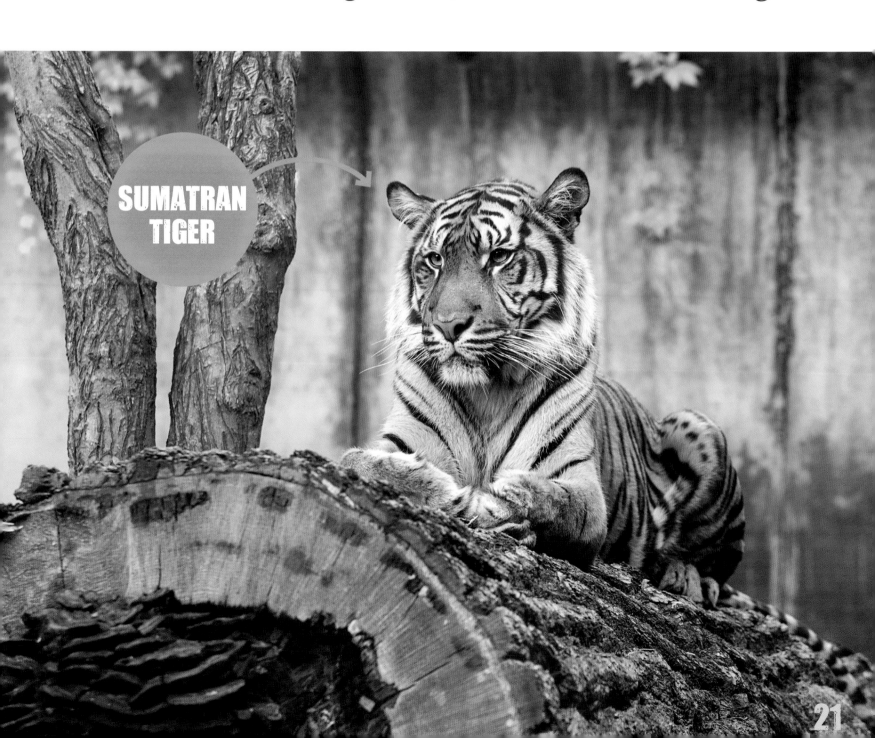

SUMATRAN TIGER

DEFORESTATION FACTS

If deforestation keeps happening as much as it is now, it is estimated that there will be no forests left within 100 years.

IF THIS HAPPENS, LOTS OF SPECIES WILL BECOME EXTINCT, LIKE THESE ORANGUTANS.

IT MIGHT TAKE HUNDREDS OF YEARS FOR ALL THE WILDLIFE TO COME BACK TO A FOREST.

Once a forest has been torn down, it can take hundreds of years for it to grow back. It may never look how it once did because it will have to grow differently.

GLOSSARY

acid rain	rain that is made acidic by pollution in the atmosphere
chemicals	substances that materials are made from
contaminated	when something has been made harmful or poisonous
environment	the natural world
extinction	when a species of animal no longer exists
fertilise	to give the soil the things it needs to grow certain plants
greenhouse gases	gases in the air that trap the Sun's heat
habitats	the natural environments in which animals or plants live
horizontal	going across instead of up and down
species	a group of very similar animals or plants that are capable of producing young together
sustainable	able to be remade or have more created of something

INDEX

carbon dioxide 13, 18–19
coal 5, 13
disasters 10–11, 20–21

environment 8, 10, 17, 19
forests 8–9, 15, 21–23
global warming 19–20
greenhouse gases 13, 19

harmful 9–11, 18
material 4–7, 10, 13
species 19, 21–22
trees 9, 14, 16, 18